This book belongs to ★

Saadie

·SONG·
·OF·THE·
EARTH·

For our children,

Sarah-Rhiannon, Rebecca, Jessica, Clara, Ellen and Joseph,

and for all the others who will inherit the Earth

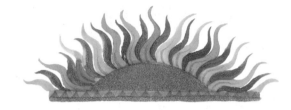

First published in Great Britain in 1995
Published in paperback in 1996,
by Orion Children's Books
a division of the Orion Publishing Group Ltd
Orion House
5 Upper St Martin's Lane
London WC2H 9EA

A catalogue record for this book is available from the British Library
Printed in Italy
ISBN 1 85881 341 7

· SONG ·
· OF · THE ·
EARTH ·

MARY HOFFMAN

Illustrated by

JANE RAY

Contents

Introduction

The song of the Earth has been sung since the beginning of time, but we can no longer hear it. Through exploring the magic of earth, fire, water and air, the words of that song may return to us and perhaps we can learn the tune again. Most of us, living in our centrally-heated homes with their modern kitchens and bathrooms, are out of touch with the four elements and never see their links with nature. Yet earth, fire, water and air still hold strong magic and are the key to a rich world of stories, legends, pictures and music.

People who lived thousands of years ago were in much closer touch with the four "elements" of life. That word, "elements", was first used to describe earth, fire, water and air 2,500 years ago, by a man named Empedocles, who lived in Greece. In his time you could not take the elements for granted. They were matters of life and death, just as they still are in many parts of the world.

Everyone needed fertile earth to grow their food crops and give grass for their animals to eat, so they believed in a great Mother Goddess who gave birth to everything that grew. But without water the crops and grass couldn't grow, so there were ceremonies and spells to make the rain come. Drinking water had to be fetched from springs and wells which were so important that people believed each one had its own god. Fire was a precious thing, to be kept alight in people's homes, to give not only warmth but light and heat for cooking. The secret of making fire was one of the things that made people different from animals. And air was the most mysterious element of all. Everyone needed it in order to live and yet they could not see it; it was somehow connected with the sky, where all the gods lived and the winds, their servants.

Empedocles didn't write just about the elements outside us. He believed that people, animals and objects were all composed of a mixture of two or more elements. His ideas were accepted for hundreds of years. In the Middle Ages, in Europe, people still believed in the presence of the four elements in human beings.

Your personality, or "humour", depended on which element had the upper hand. So a "fiery" person would be quick-tempered and ambitious, an "airy" one would be creative and cheerful, an "earthy" one placid and reliable, and a "watery" one thoughtful and inclined to be sad. All twelve signs of the Zodiac are assigned to one of the elements, three to each. Earth signs, for example, are Taurus, Virgo and Capricorn. If you are born "under" one of these signs, in certain dates in the year, you are supposed to have "earthy" characteristics.

You don't have to believe in any of this to find it fascinating. Myths, legends, riddles, proverbs and superstitions expressing beliefs about the four elements lie deep in the art and literature of the West and there are interesting and exciting beliefs about the elements in many other cultures. We have included stories and images from cultures which do not share in the Western tradition of four elements. Some belief systems divide the world into two, like the Chinese concept of Yin and Yang. Water and earth are Yin, or female, while air and fire are the masculine Yang forces.

There is such a rich world of ideas and images connected with the four elements that there is too much for one book. But here you can explore in words and pictures at least some of the power and mystery, the exhilaration and the danger of being close to the four elements.

Human beings have so lost touch with the elements that they haven't noticed what "advanced" cultures are doing to them. We have poisoned the earth, polluted the water and air with our chemicals and industries, and used fire to lay waste acres of rainforest and grazing ground - all in the name of progress.

We should try to recapture a sense of wonder at these four elements of life. If people feel closer to the earth, they will feel more reverence for trees and every growing thing. If they respect fire, they will not use it so destructively. If they recognize the life-giving qualities of water, they will be ashamed to dump their rubbish into rivers and seas. If they believe that the air is the source of all life they will try harder to keep it clean and good to breathe.

As you discover the thrill of volcanoes and earthquakes, the mystery of drowned cities and the beauty of legends about rainbows and Starpeople, you can join in celebrating the magic of Earth, Fire, Water and Air. You can join in the song of the Earth.

Mother Earth

Earth is the first and most important element. The Greeks and Romans named our planet after it; in the Middle Ages it was seen as the central element of the four. It is easy to see why many people thought of the earth as their first mother, the source of all life. The Greeks called her Gaia; she was Prithivi to the Hindus and Ishtar to the Babylonians. People all over the world, from North America to Japan, Scandinavia to New Zealand, believed in an earth mother-goddess and a sky-father. Only in Ancient Egypt was it the other way round - Geb was the earth-god and Nut the sky-goddess.

Women who wanted babies and women who were about to give birth pressed themselves close to the ground to share in her fruitfulness. Until quite recently, in one part of Italy, newborn babies were placed on the earth as soon as they had been bathed and dressed. It was a way of saying that all life comes from the earth our mother.

All the food that people eat either grows from the soil or comes from animals, who themselves rely on the earth to provide their food. Even the birds of the air and fishes of the sea depend on food which comes from the earth.

Gradually, though, we seem to have forgotten that the earth is the mother of us all.

Life in the dark

The earth is a generous mother. She gives shelter to many kinds of animals in her warm embrace. Some of the most humble are the most important, like the common earthworm. Earth passes through its body as it passes through the earth, breaking up the soil as it goes, making it crumbly and diggable.

Bigger animals make tunnels under the earth, forming intricate patterns, like the warrens of rabbits, the underground labyrinths of meerkats and moles, mongooses and badgers. These are the places where they sleep, give birth and hide from predators.

But it is not just animals who burrow and tunnel into the earth. In the Ice Age people lived in underground caves. Caves have been found in France painted with the images of bison and antelope and all the other animals that Ice Age people hunted for food. These painted caves were magical places where young boys were brought when they came of age to become hunters.

Thousands of years later, people found out that the earth-mother had many treasures hidden inside her - gold, silver, diamonds and coal - which could only be seized from her by those who would go down into the dark. She takes many lives in return for the riches people dig out of her.

The earth has her own creatures, special to her, the earthbound ones who cannot fly or swim. Above all others, the bull symbolizes the strength and solidity of the earth, and carries its own magic. Even today, conjurors still use the word "Abracadabra", which comes from an ancient phrase meaning "the bull, the only bull", when they want to create a magical illusion.

BUFFALO DUSK

The buffaloes are gone.
And those who saw the buffaloes are gone.
Those who saw the buffaloes by thousands and how they pawed the
     prairie sod into dust with their hoofs, their great heads down
     pawing on in a great pageant of dusk,
Those who saw the buffaloes are gone.
And the buffaloes are gone.

Carl Sandburg

Earth's animals, the large meat-eaters and the animals they feed on, the hoofed and
the horned, take up a lot of room. But the open spaces are shrinking and the animals
are disappearing too.

As if the earth did not throw up enough wonderful creatures naturally, myth and legend have given us even more miraculous beasts. The unicorn might be an elegant interpretation of the rhinoceros, by people who had only heard about it, or it might be a result of the belief that everything on the land had its counterpart in the sea. When spiralled narwhal horns were washed up on beaches, people of the Middle Ages deduced there must be a single-horned animal on the earth too.

The centaur was a creature of Greek myth, a man down to the waist, fused with the body of a horse. It came into being because people had seen men riding horses for the first time and could not believe their eyes.

The Sphinx was made up of bits of other animals. The Greek Sphinx has a woman's head and breasts, the body of a lion, the wings of an eagle and a serpent's tail. The Egyptian Sphinx has a lion's body and the head of a man.

There was only ever one Chimaera, an incredible three-headed mixture of lion, dragon and she-goat. It terrorized the people of Lycia in Asia Minor until it was killed by Bellerophon.

The earth is not always a gentle and loving mother; sometimes she can be terrifying and destructive. Suddenly, often without warning, the ground begins to shake and rumble and the earth splits open, swallowing anything that gets in the way.

Some earthquakes strike in remote,
uninhabited places - even under the sea.
But others attack crowded cities like Los
Angeles and Tokyo. It is becoming possible
to predict earthquakes and to make buildings
earthquake-proof. But even in earlier times,
when there was no chance of avoiding or
predicting earthquakes, people would always
come back and build again in the same spot.

The one thing that the fruitful earth cannot produce is living creatures, though many legends say she can. One of them tells of the Greek hero Cadmus, who made men spring out of the earth. When he arrived in the land where he was to found the city of Thebes, he tried to drink some water from a spring. He did not realize that it was sacred to the war god Ares, who had put a huge dragon to guard it. Cadmus killed the dragon, so that he could drink, and Ares never forgave him.

Then the goddess Athene, who had been watching, told Cadmus to take the teeth of the dragon and plant them in the earth like seeds. When he obeyed her, a host of armed warriors immediately sprang up, too many for Cadmus to command. He threw a stone among them and they quarrelled over who had thrown it, killing one another till there were only five left. These five followed Cadmus for the rest of his life.

Earth to earth

Perhaps because of a lingering belief that the earth could bring life to anything, people have buried their dead for almost as long as there have been people on earth. If she could bring back flowers and crops and trees after the dead period of winter, perhaps mother earth could bring her human children back to life too.

The Christian burial service still says "Earth to earth, ashes to ashes, dust to dust; in sure and certain hope of the Resurrection to eternal life."

The Celts piled the earth high into burial mounds on top of their kings and warriors. The ancient Egyptians carried the idea of burial mounds even further. They constructed huge pyramids for their kings, the Pharaohs, and buried them in chambers deep inside. They made sure that the Pharaoh had all his favourite possessions buried with him, along with food and wine to keep him going on his way in the afterlife.

The cycle of the seasons

Life comes back out of the earth every spring and many myths and legends around the world arise from attempts to explain this annual miracle. The Greeks had a corn-goddess Demeter who was the granddaughter of great mother earth herself. She had a daughter, called Persephone, whose father was Zeus, the king of the gods. Persephone was stolen by Hades, the god of the Underworld, to be his wife. Demeter made Zeus get her daughter back for her. But because Persephone got hungry and ate six pomegranate seeds when she was in the Underworld, she can live on the earth for only six months of the year. During the other six months she has to go back to Hades. Her mother misses her so much that the leaves fall off the trees and the earth is as bleak and miserable as Demeter feels. And that is one explanation of the seasons.

Because most trees seem to die in the winter and come back to life in the spring, they have always seemed magical, symbols of everlasting life.

"Trees, eternal attempts by the earth
To speak to the listening sky."
Rabindranath Tagore

And many trees do live for hundreds of years, much longer than people. Because a tree has its roots in the earth but reaches its branches high up into the sky, it is also a symbol of striving for higher and better things. To the Celts the oak-tree was sacred, for Indians it was the fig-tree. The people of the north, where the Vikings came from, believed that the whole world was supported by a great ash-tree. Its name was Yggdrasil. At the bottom, coiled round its roots, there lay a dragon, the Nidhogg, and at the top was an eagle. Ratatösk the squirrel scurried between them, carrying insults from one to the other. Yggdrasil's roots went down into Niflheim and up into Asgard where the gods lived. It had been there for ever and would never die.

Saving the earth

If the earth is our mother, we have treated her very badly. We have moved a long way from the native North American who refused even to dig in the earth, saying that it would mean wounding his mother. Now many parts of the world that were once full of trees have become deserts where nothing grows and nothing can live.

Large areas of rainforest in the Amazon, Madagascar, Rwanda and other places have been burned or cut down. Sometimes this is to make money for rich companies, but often people need the land for farming and cannot afford to do things more slowly or think about the future; they need food for their families now. Around the world so much is being lost - wildlife and its habitat, traditional ways of life - that it seems time is running out for many of the treasures of the earth, unless countries can work together to preserve them.

But the solutions to big problems often begin with something small. In India the Chipko movement began when women in a village put their arms round the trees which were about to be cut down to make way for a factory. They told the woodcutters they would have to saw through them too. The women had seen how cutting down lots of trees led to floods which washed away roads and bridges. Now the Chipko (hug-the-tree) movement has spread all over India. It is a case of ordinary people making a real change to what is happening to the earth.

FIRE

Round the fire

The secret of making fire is one of the gifts that make people different from animals. We can summon fire as we wish and make it cook for us, keep us warm, even destroy for us if we want it to. But you may live all your life in a modern house and never see a flame.

Yet there is something special about firelight and candlelight. It takes us back to a time when fire warded off the wild creatures and the even wilder demons we imagined howling for us in the dark. Everyone loves a log fire, a campfire, a bonfire. Candles in a church symbolize the soul. We make a wish when we blow out our birthday candles, perhaps to celebrate surviving for another year. When you see a candle flame struggling to do battle with the dark and being consumed, it is easier to understand the symbolism of light and dark, than when you press an electric switch.

Fire mountains

Fire is not always tame and comforting. There are stories of twinkling fires, called will o' the wisps, leading people to their deaths in the marshes. When fire is out of control, it can be the most terrifying of the four elements. Forest fires that get out of hand leave nothing standing in their path.

The most fearsome of all
natural fires comes from the heart
of a volcano. The Hindus of Java
believe that a god lives inside the Fire
Mountain, which is what they call the
volcano. They can grow three crops of rice a year
from the fertile soil on the volcano's slopes, full of ash
from old eruptions. Even if their fire mountain has erupted
quite recently, they still climb up to the crater every year to throw
in offerings to the god, in thanks for the rich harvest. People always
want to live on and near volcanoes, because the land is good, even though
they never know when the air will be suddenly filled with fire and boiling lava.

Night-fires

There is nothing quite so magical as the contrast between a bright light and the night sky. The first night-fires were the moon and stars, and there are enough stories about them to fill many books. If you look at the sky on a clear night at the right time of year, you can see some of the signs of the Zodiac, such as the Crab, the Bull and the Water-carrier. You can see Greek heroes, such as Orion, the hunter, and Perseus, who killed the Medusa, animals like Pegasus and the Great Bear, and women as beautiful as their names - Andromeda, Cassiopeia and the Pleiades.

The Dragon constellation, named by the Babylonians, is sixteen stars arranged round the Pole Star - you can see it in the north in spring, coiled forever round the Little Bear and hissing at Hercules. The night sky is a living storybook.

We like to add our own fires to the night sky. The ancient religions of Britain used fires at festivals for grisly sacrificial reasons. These are now converted to firework displays and bonfires and jack o' lanterns. But whenever there is a really big celebration, such as Chinese New Year, there must be fireworks to dazzle our eyes and lift our spirits.

Fire Worship

The first people to make fire lived in China about 400,000 years ago. That may seem a long time, but it is recent in human history compared with the other three elements. Earth, water and air are all around us but fire occurs naturally only occasionally. Perhaps this accounts for the importance of fire in ancient mythologies.

In many parts of the world the first gods to be worshipped were Sun-gods, powerful fire-beings who lived inside the sun. The supreme god of the Egyptians was Ra, who shared his qualities with whoever was king at the time. In India, Surya, "the eye of heaven", and Savitri were both sun gods. Parsees of Iran and India still worship Ahura-Mazda and have sacred ceremonies involving flames.

Sun gods are usually male. Because the sun disappears down into the dark at each dusk and rises with the dawn each morning, many people believed in a fiery god who died every night and overcame the powers of darkness to come back to life every morning. Ra, for example, steered across the heavens in a boat, pursued by a huge crocodile, who seemed to devour the sun at the end of the day. The reappearance of the sun in the morning was a sign that Ra had killed the crocodile once more.

Stealing fire

There are many stories about how people found out how to make fire from the gods or who-ever else was its keeper. The native Americans in what is now Canada told a story that it was Bear who had the secret of fire. He kept a firestone tied to his belt and used it to make sparks.

One day when he was relaxing in his cave in front of a fire, a cold little bird hopped in and

asked to be warmed. The gruff bear consented - in return for the bird picking lice out of his fur. This she did, but every now and again she also pecked at the thong holding the firestone. As soon as the thong was pecked through, she snatched the stone and flew away. Outside the cave, a long line of animals passed the magic stone along as quickly as in a game of pass the parcel. The last one was Fox. He ran to the top of a mountain and dashed the stone in pieces. He threw a fragment to each of the tribes. And that is how North Americans learned how to make fire.

Fire has its own mythical creatures. The legendary salamander was able to live unharmed inside a fire. The Egyptian phoenix was an extraordinary bird which represented the sun - there was only one at any time. It was a beautiful bird with red and gold feathers, which lived for a thousand years. When the time came for it to die, it built its own funeral pyre out of spiced wood and the sun's rays set fire to it. A new phoenix was born from the ashes of the fire symbolising new life and hope.

The fire-creature we know best is the dragon . There are as many stories about it as about the unicorn. Perhaps they grew out of people's glimpses of giant lizards. We all know what a traditional European dragon looks like without ever having seen one - a huge scaly serpent with wings and a long reptilian tail. It has fearsome teeth, a forked tongue and huge nostrils, out of which it breathes flame. Its traditional food is young maidens and its enemy a hero with a sword.

The eternal flame

"How many miles to Babylon?
Three score miles and ten.
Can I get there by candlelight?
Yes and back again."

Candlelight can take you to places you can only dream of. It has a magical quality, fending off the terrors of the dark, yet held in the hand like a talisman. There is traditionally something sacred about a single flame, which is why Christian churches use candles in processions and on the altar. But the tradition is older still : in ancient Rome there was a temple to the Goddess Vesta, who was in charge of the sacred flame of the hearth. She had taken a vow to remain unmarried all her life. The young women who came and served in her temple followed her example and were known as Vestal Virgins. The single flame is a symbol of a single soul. That is why Catholics light candles for the souls of the dead and why eternal flames are kept burning on the many tombs of the unknown warrior, memorials to the unnamed soldiers who have fought and died in wars. When the Olympic Games begin every four years, the high point of the opening ceremony is the bringing in of the torch to ignite the Olympic flame; this will be kept burning throughout the games.

In many places in the Mediterranean there are processions up to high places of worship to celebrate Easter. They are held in the warm flower-scented dark, with every person in the village or town climbing the hill with their torches and candles. At midnight on Easter Saturday, the vigil comes to an end with the lighting of the huge Paschal Candle, from which small ones are lit, to celebrate the Resurrection on Easter Sunday.

The big important moments of birth and death are when people feel closest to the elements. Like earth, fire has a part to play in the rituals surrounding death. Hindus build funeral pyres and have strong beliefs about which member of the dead person's family should light the fires. Viking heroes were launched out to sea on their ships, which were set fire to as the ship slipped into the water. Only a very great warrior or chieftain was treated in this way, since the ships were of great value; the dead man's richest belongings were destroyed with him.

At the burial of the Norse god Balder, his horse was slaughtered and thrown into the ship. Balder's wife, who had died of a broken heart, was burnt with him.

It may seem a long way from a Viking hero's funeral, but many people today also have their bodies burned, or cremated, when they die. It takes up far less room to bury a person's ashes than their whole body. Some people even ask for their ashes to be scattered in a place they loved in their lifetime.

Fire is supposed to be
"a good servant but a bad master".
In other words, we enjoy all the warmth and comfort
and cooked food that depend on fire but are terrified of it
when it gets out of hand. Perhaps this is because we have never
really had mastery of it. Even the planned burning of woodland
and forests has results beyond human control. The fertile topsoil
can disappear once the trees have gone, and gradually the land
becomes a desert where nothing grows.

But the old idea of fire living in the sun gives us new hope for the
planet too. The energy which comes from the sun can be used instead
of burning trees and the coal that comes from the fossils of trees.
Solar energy can warm our homes and heat our water and perhaps
cook our food. So we have found a new way to come close
to one of the traditional spirits of fire.

The sea

Human beings are made of nearly three-quarters water and the Earth itself has twice as much water as land. Perhaps this is why we are so fascinated by the sea. Its water is undrinkable to humans, but it yields a fine crop of food to anyone brave enough to risk its unpredictable moods. Whether lying calm and sparkling under the sun, or towering in terrifying waves, the sea draws us to it. It has given birth to more stories, poems, superstitions and works of art and music than perhaps any other element. From ancient times, the desire to explore its vast expanses and deeps has led to perilous adventures.

Herodotus wrote 2,500 years ago, "There are the living, the dead, and those who voyage on the sea."

Living
water

Unlike the sea, all forms of falling water are fresh and drinkable. The waterfall, which occurs naturally, has been copied and turned into the dam for practical use and the fountain for ornament and refreshment. When the Muslims invaded India hundreds of years ago, they brought with them their love of water, and their dynasty of kings in India encouraged the making of water-gardens. There is hardly a city or town in the world that doesn't have its public fountains, endlessly recycling water in sprays and arcs from elaborate sculptures. It may be that this is a modern day tribute to the idea of "the fountain of youth" or "the water of life", going back to some very ancient beliefs about creation. Moving water, in springs and waterfalls, was thought to be "living water" and therefore able to give life or restore youth.

ater is a female element, like earth. It is closely associated with fertility and childbirth. In Mexico, the washing of newborn babies was accompanied by chants to the water-goddess who was celebrated as the child's real mother. Early ancestors of the Finns and Hungarians prayed to a water-mother for babies. And in the Gambia in the present day, women with fertility problems will visit sacred crocodile pools and bathe themselves with the water, before praying to be given children.

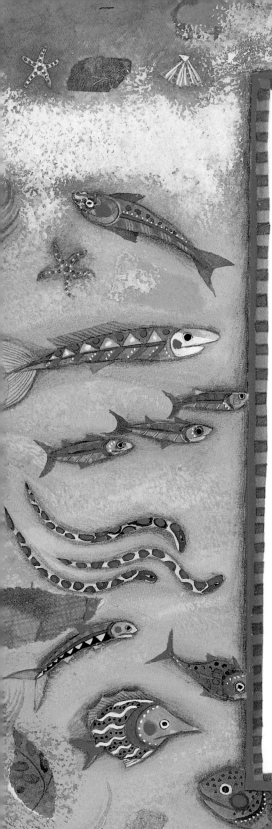

Fishes

There is something very mysterious about creatures that can live in the element of water. Some, like fishes, can breathe underwater and spend their whole lives there. To them our element of air means death. Others, the mammals from whales to walruses, have to come up for air eventually. But apart from that, they are perfectly adapted to their element, having sleek bodies and powerful muscles so that they can swim as well as fish. Sharks never sleep; their whole lives are spent on the move in the water.

"The tiny fish enjoy themselves
in the sea.
Quick little splinters of life,
their little lives are fun to them
in the sea."
D.H.Lawrence

Miracles

The Bible is full of water miracles, in both the Old Testament and the New, and they feature both salt and fresh water. When the Israelites were escaping from the Egyptians who had made slaves of them, they came to a halt at the edge of the Red Sea. Then Jehovah divided the water, just like a comb parting hair and kept the waves back till all the Israelites had crossed safely to the other side. He let the sea fall back, and all the Egyptians were drowned.

One of Jesus's first miracles was to turn water into wine at a wedding feast. Another time he walked on the water in Lake Galilee and showed his disciples where to cast their fishing nets to pull up an amazing haul of fish. Power over the slippery element of water is a sign of a great hero or leader.

Holy water

The Unicorn is also said to have power over water. It can cleanse the most poisonous and polluted water by dipping its long horn into it. Native North Americans along with many other peoples tried to gain power over water by chanting and performing ritual dances to make the rain come. A Navajo rainchant begins:

> Far as man can see,
>   Comes the rain,
>   Comes the rain with me.
>
> From the Rain-Mount,
>   Rain-Mount far away,
>   Comes the rain,
>   Comes the rain with me.

When the rain did come, it must have seemed a real miracle.

Many religions still use water as part of their ceremonies. In the Christian church, new members are baptized with holy water; they may be completely submerged in a small pool. Dipping in water symbolizes the old life being washed away and a new life beginning.

In India, the whole of the long river Ganges is regarded as sacred by the Hindus. Washing in its waters is supposed to be lucky, particularly at the holy city of Benares. But even though the river is holy, people still wash their clothes and themselves in it. Rubbish is emptied into the river and bodies are floated down it. The spirit of the Ganges is supposed to be great enough to cope with any pollution.

Mermaids

There are many stories of creatures living in the water who are stranger than any real ones. The most persistent is that of the mermaid. According to tradition, she is a beautiful young woman, with golden hair and a comb and mirror, but from the waist down all fish. She is the downfall of many sailors, enticing them into deep water with her singing. The whole idea of mermaids probably originated from sailors' tales of the dugong, a sea-mammal which suckles its young in an upright position in the water. So the image of the lovely and seductive mermaid may come from a rather homely sea-cow.

Greek legends are full of stories of tritons and sea-nymphs ruled over by the great god Poseidon, with his long beard and trident. There were monsters too, like the one who was going to eat the princess Andromeda till Perseus the hero rescued her. The belief in water monsters is still common. Many people still think there is a monster in Loch Ness.

Floods

Water is so unpredictable and so frightening when it has been whipped up by storms that it is easy to see where the idea of sea-monsters comes from. Storms and torrential rains are as destructive as fire and can move as fast. Tidal waves, caused by undersea earthquakes and volcanoes, travel with horrific speed and crash on to the land, killing people and animals and ruining whole cities.

Many countries all over the world have stories of a Great Flood that wiped out all the people on earth except one family.

From them the earth had a fresh start and a whole new race of people was born. This story is so common that some historians think there was once such a universal flooding. The earliest version comes in an inscription from about 4,000 years ago in Mesopotamia, in which the survivor was not an ordinary good man like Noah, but a great king called Ziusudra. He dreamed that the gods were cursing the earth and so he built a boat.

"All the windstorms of immense power, they all came together.
The rainstorm raged along with them.
And when for seven days and seven nights
The rainstorm in the land had raged,
The huge boat on the great waters by the windstorm had been carried away,
Utu, the sun, came forth, shedding light over heaven and earth....."

Drowned Atlantis

Whether or not there was a flood over the whole world, there were certainly many disturbances in the waters of the Mediterranean in ancient times. Earthquakes and volcanoes led to tidal waves, one of which is famous for overwhelming the city of Atlantis.

For a long time the story of lost Atlantis, a great city under the water, seemed to be just a myth, based on an Egyptian story that was later written down by the Greek philosopher Plato. His portrait of the island kingdom of Atlantis was very detailed, describing the main city of this great civilization as built on a hilltop surrounded by three circles of seawater and two of land. According to Plato, the island had been given to the god Poseidon, whose sons ruled there for generations. It was a great power, rich in crops and trade and possessing a strong army.

Then suddenly, in the course of a day and a night, the whole island was destroyed and its civilization wiped out as if it had never been.

Archaeologists have found remains on the Aegean island of Santorini which show that a great Minoan city once prospered there. It was destroyed in 1500 BC by an earthquake, which sent tidal waves as far as north Crete. There were even concentric rings found under the sea near the island. It does seem as if Atlantis might have been a real place after all.

There is no kind of water which cannot be polluted by modern life. Our rivers, lakes, pools and sea alike have been contaminated. Even the rain that falls from the sky in some places has so many chemicals in it that trees are dying.

Sometimes something that seemed a good idea and a benefit to people, such as fertilizers to help food grow in poor earth, has led to water-pollution, as chemicals have washed off the land and into the rivers. Oil-slicks in the sea have killed wildlife and left a sticky black mess on our beaches. But slowly people are remembering how precious clean water is, and laws have been made to prevent dumping at sea.

Some businesses have even started collecting rainwater in huge barrels, just as people used to a hundred years ago, to reduce the amount of water they use from reservoirs.

The Greeks must have spent a lot of time looking up at the sky. They told many stories of heroes who tried to conquer the air. One of them was a young man called Bellerophon. The goddess Athene helped him to catch a wonderful flying horse called Pegasus. Bellerophon did great deeds with the help of the winged horse but in the end he got too ambitious and tried to fly up to the gods' home on Mount Olympus.

Zeus decided to teach him a lesson. He sent a gadfly to sting Pegasus, so that the horse shied and threw Bellerophon to earth. Pegasus reached Olympus and lived there ever after.

Icarus was another young man who tried to fly. His father Daedalus was a prisoner on the island of Crete and he made them both wings, so that they could escape by air. Daedalus warned his son not to fly too close to the sun, but once he felt the air under his wings, Icarus forgot. The hot sun melted the wax that held the feathers together. His wings fell apart and he plunged to his death in the sea.

Iris was the messenger of the gods. A rainbow was her stairway in the air from Olympus to earth.

The home of the gods

The rainbow played a
part in Norse mythology
too. The people of the north believed
there was a rainbow bridge between
middle earth, where people lived, and Asgard,
which was the home of the gods. Across it might
come Thor, the mighty thunder-god, who made
storms by whirling his hammer; or perhaps Odin, the
chief god, known as the Allfather.

Odin was a great sky god. He rode an eight-legged horse called Sleipnir and had two pet ravens whose names meant Thought and Memory. They flew through the air carrying messages to and from the Allfather.

Odin built a great palace in Asgard called Valhalla. The Valkyries did his bidding there. They were powerful warrior-women who flew through the skies above battlefields, collecting dead heroes to bring back to Valhalla, to make a strong army to defend Odin against his enemies.

Thunderbirds and Starpeople

In North America, the people of the lakes and plains looked up at the magnificent golden eagles and other birds that whirled through the air and thought they must be winged spirits. The Algonquins believed that birds caused the winds by the beating of their wings. The tribes of the northwest believed in winged gods called Thunderbirds - they thought that lightning was the flash of a Thunderbird's eye.

Many native North Americans believed in a Star Country where beautiful beings lived way above the earth. Sometimes a Starmaiden would spy a handsome brave and come down to earth in disguise. She would take him back up to her own country. Sometimes it was the beauty of a mortal woman which caught the eye of one of the Star-youths. But the story always ended the same way.

The Starpeople could marry mortals and have children with them. All was well as long as the humans lived up in the Star Country with their loved ones. But they eventually got homesick and wanted to revisit their own people. Even then all would have been well if they had only kept their life with the Starpeople a secret. They were always tempted into telling and then they could never go back.

Winged creatures

Everyone can imagine how wonderful it must be to have wings and be able to fly. But for the creatures that do, life is hard; they spend most of their time searching for food. A little bird must eat several times its own body-weight every day to stay alive. Big birds like hawks and owls have to catch fast-moving little creatures to eat.

There are thousands of different kinds of birds, from the hedge sparrow to the giant condor, and there are millions of different kinds of insects. Many of them can fly too. Butterflies, dragonflies, damselflies, bees and ladybirds all live a very short life compared with people, and they spend most of it on the wing. Within days, sometimes within hours, they must eat, mate and leave eggs to grow into more winged creatures like themselves.

Perhaps it is because people can fly only in their minds that we have invented so many creatures with wings. The angels and archangels of Christianity are powerful and frightening, like stern Michael with his flaming sword standing guard at the gate of Eden to stop Adam and Eve getting back in. Less frightening are the chubby little boy cherubs that painters of five hundred years ago put into their pictures of Jesus and his mother. Smaller than cherubs are tiny creatures with butterfly wings who are the fairies of fairy stories.

But the devil was an angel once too - Lucifer, the light bringer - and there are many other imaginary winged creatures that are wicked, like the vampire Count Dracula. The demon Ravana, who stole Sita from Rama in the Hindu story of the Ramayana, had ten heads and twenty arms. Rama managed to track him down and kill him, with the help of another air spirit, the great bird, Jatayu.

Red sky at night

The one aspect of the elements that every person is still in touch with is the weather. For some it is a vital question of rain to make crops grow or fair weather for safe sea-fishing, for others just a matter of taking an umbrella or hoping for sunshine on the beach. But we all look up at the sky and sense in the air what the weather is going to be like today.

Meteorologists use very sophisticated instruments and calculations for predicting the weather, but they so often get it wrong that we may prefer the traditional custom of foretelling the weather from whether a piece of seaweed feels damp or dry.

There are many little sayings about the weather, mostly based on the look of the sky. Some of these actually fit in with scientific explanations about cloud-formations, but they were all based on observations, handed down over generations, long before there was any science of meteorology.

A rainbow in the morning is a sailor's warning
A rainbow at night is a sailor's delight.

When clouds appear like rocks and towers,
The earth's refreshed by frequent showers.

If woolly fleeces spread the heavenly way,
No rain, be sure, disturbs the summer's day.

Evening red and morning grey,
Help the traveller on his way.
Evening grey and morning red,
Bring down rain upon his head.

When the wind is in the North,
The skilful fisher goes not forth.
When the wind is in the East,
It is neither good for man nor beast.
When the wind is in the South,
It blows your bait into a fish's mouth.
When the wind is in the West,
Then the weather is at its best.

Red sky at night, shepherd's delight.
Red sky in the morning, shepherd's warning.

Mackerel scales and mare's tails
Make lofty ships carry low sails.

Hurricanes
and tornadoes

The air around us can become as horrific as
any other of the four elements if we live in countries
where there are hurricanes and typhoons. These are
violent tropical storms with winds that travel up to
220 miles per hour (360 kph). What begins as a small
thunderstorm out over the warm ocean builds up into
a spinning circle sucking up warm air. By the time it
reaches land, it is an outer circle of devastating winds
with a calm "eye" at the centre.

Tornadoes, or whirlwinds, move even faster than hurricanes. They can cause terrible destruction in minutes, hurling trees, roofs and even people up into the air and carrying them long distances before flinging them down again. The tornado starts in a storm, when warm air is sucked up into a column of swirling wind. A long funnel of twisting air hangs down from the thundercloud and when it touches the earth, the powerful vacuum sucks up everything in its path.

A breath of fresh air

Air is the most easily polluted element of all. Contained in a small room it can quickly fill up with smoke from cigarettes or fumes from aerosol sprays. Out in the open, in the vastness of the sky, it is hard to believe that the air cannot somehow clean itself. Since it cannot, there is now a hole in the protective layer of ozone that covers the earth, appearing over the Antarctic every spring. The ozone layer protects us from the harmful rays of the sun that cause skin cancer, so it is very important to stop that hole getting any bigger. We have to respect the air around us - try to use our cars less, try not to use aerosols with CFCs, recycle our rubbish instead of burning it, make smoking tobacco a thing of the past and campaign to stop the rainforests being cut down.

If we listen to the song of the Earth, we can have a closer and more harmonious relationship with the elements. We can remember how vital earth, fire, water and air are to human life. We can acknowledge what powerful influences they have been on people in the past and what great art they have inspired. And with every small step to help one of the four elements a little is put back of the magic they have lost. One day, if we learn to treat them as friends, not enemies, Earth, Fire, Water and Air may regain the natural power they had when the world began.